Wilma, the Resurrection Bunny

Juanita G. Ellis
Illustrated by Sharon B. Parker

LSKIDSTUFF

Colorful, Creative, Christian Teaching Materials for Children

www.lskidstuff.com

Wilma, the Resurrection Bunny
ISBN: Softcover 978-1-946478-66-5
Copyright © 2018 by Juanita Ellis

All rights reserved. No part of this book may be reproduced or transmitted in any form or by any means, electronic or mechanical, including photocopying, recording, or by any information storage and retrieval system, without permission in writing from the publisher.

Wilma, the Resurrection Bunny

Hello!

I'd like you to meet someone. Her name is Wilma.

She is a mother rabbit.

The snow is beginning to melt and is dripping down into her rabbit hole.

"We are going to leave our underground home today," Wilma told her excited babies. Over the long winter 14 little baby bunnies were born. They make the home very crowded.

Wilma decided today is the day that everyone will stick their bunny noses out into the sunshine. She dresses each one of her babies in new Spring bunny clothes.

She puts on HER new Spring dress too. She wants her children to learn some important lessons. She wants each one of her children to pronounce a HUGE word.

"All winter long the earth and plants, trees and grass have stopped growing," Wilma tells her bunnies. "Did you know that during the cold winter everything stops growing? Many plants die during the winter cold."

She showed her family some small buds starting to burst open. Wilma showed Frannie, one of the bunny twins, the strawberry vine which looked so brown and dry last month.

That same strawberry vine has tiny red blooms on it! Wilma whispered something into Frannie and Annie's long rabbit ears. It is the HUGE word.

"What is the HUGE word I want my bunnies to learn?" Wilma asks. "RESURRECTION!" the babies all speak at once. Wilma told her bunnies that resurrection means life ... running, jumping, playing and hopping.

"Every Spring the cold, dead ground comes back to life. The grass, brown and dry all winter, is now green! Resurrection is a miracle. Only God can bring something which has died back to life again."

Finally, as each of the 14 white bunny tails wiggle back to their home, they feel glad a miracle of life happens every Spring. The bunnies want YOU to say "resurrection."

It is a very difficult word. The bunnies understand Spring has come to our world. The sun is warm, and the grass is green.

God loves our world

and

God loves us!

Suggestions

How to Present *Wilma, The Resurrection Bunny* to Students

- Provide a bunny piñata, stuffed animal, or hand puppet to represent Wilma.

- Place wrapped candy in the piñata. If a stuffed animal or hand puppet is used, the stuffed animal or puppet may hold a basket filled with candy.

- Before presenting Wilma, the Resurrection Bunny, wrap Wilma in colorful cellophane with a big bow. Present Wilma to the children wrapped in this colorful packaging. Unwrap in the classroom. Place candy with Wilma before wrapping.

- Before class, prepare a small Easter basket for each child complete with colorful grass. A small plastic cup makes a good basket. Add ribbon for a handle.

- Wilma is a story to celebrate the arrival of Spring. However, Wilma is particularly intended as an aid to the Easter message, the resurrection of the Lord Jesus.

- Each child reaching into Wilma's cache and filling their hands with goodies. This is Wilma, the Resurrection Bunny.

May you and your students
enjoy her for many years
to come!

Wilma, the Resurrection Bunny

A Puppet Show

Narrator: Hello! I'd like for you to meet someone. Her name is Wilma. She is a Mother rabbit. The snow is beginning to melt and is dripping down into her rabbit hole. Over the long winter 14 little baby bunnies were born. They make the home very crowded. "Shhh. Wilma is talking to her baby bunnies right now."

Wilma: "We are going to take a walk outside today. All of my baby bunnies must wear their new Spring bunny clothes."

Action: Baby bunnies jumping up and down with joy.

Narrator: Wilma has decided to put on HER new Spring dress too. She wants her children to learn some important lessons. She wants each one of her bunnies to pronounce a HUGE word.

Whisper. "I think Wilma is dressing each of her children in their Spring clothes right now. Let's watch. Maybe we will see some bunny noses peeking out into the warm sunshine."

Action: Each bunny puppet should now be wearing a small, decorated Easter hat tied under the chin. One by one the bunny hats, and bunny noses, show themselves little by little until they are fully visible.

Wilma: "Did you know that during the winter everything stops growing? Many plants die during the winter cold."

Action: Wilma shows her family some small buds starting to burst open.

Frannie and Annie, two of the bunny twins, speak excitedly while peering at a small patch of greenery with smidgens of red. "Look! The strawberry vine has tiny red blooms on it!" All the other bunny siblings gather round the blooms, smelling and ohhhing.

Narrator: Look! Wilma is whispering something into each one of her baby's long rabbit ears. What do you think she is whispering? (Pause.) It's the **HUGE** word!

Action: Wilma whispers into each puppet ear.

Wilma: "What is the HUGE word I want my bunnies to say?"

Action: "RESURRECTION!" the babies all speak at once, jumping up and down.

Wilma: "Do each of my bunnies know what resurrection means?"

Action: Wilma waits, looking around.

Wilma: "Resurrection means life ... running, jumping, playing and hopping. Every Spring the cold ground comes back to life. The dry, brown grass is green again! Resurrection is a miracle. Only God can bring a miracle."

Narrator: As each of the 14 white bunny tails wiggle back to their home, they feel glad they know a miracle of life happens every Spring. The bunnies want YOU to say "resurrection." It is a very difficult word. Can you say "resurrection?"

Audience: "Resurrection!"

Narrator: The bunnies understand that Spring has come to our world. The sun is warm. The grass is green. God loves our world and God loves us!

Action: Baby bunnies jumping up and down with joy.

www.ingramcontent.com/pod-product-compliance
Lightning Source LLC
Chambersburg PA
CBHW081400080526
44588CB00016B/2562